Karri —
you are
such a great
designer and
you are Bound to
success — Raising
the bar always —

♡ Donn

D0361796

POCKET *for* POSITIVES

SUCCESS

POCKET POSITIVES
for
SUCCESS

An Anthology of Quotations

Summit Press
950 Stud Road, Rowville
Victoria 3178
Australia

Email: publishing@fivemile.com.au
Website: www.fivemile.com.au

First published 2000 as *The Complete Pocket Positives*
This revised edition first published 2006

Compiled by Maggie Pinkney
Designed by Zoë Murphy
Illustration by Kieran Murphy
Printed in China

ISBN 1 74178 000 4

CONTENTS

Make the Most of Your Mistakes

Just Do It!

Never Give Up

Face Up to Fear

Opportunities Are for Taking

Genius or Hard Work?

You Can Do More Than You Think You Can...

Cherish Your Friends

Secrets of Success

PREFACE

Success comes in many shapes. To some people it's synonymous with fame and fortune. To others it means improving social conditions for the underprivileged, achieving excellence in a particular field or simply creating something beautiful. But no matter what their personal aspirations, there's a common denominator in the qualities possessed by all successful individuals. Firstly, they have a dream. Secondly, they believe in themselves. And finally, they're prepared to work. Extremely hard.

A recurring theme in this unique anthology is the importance of being able to learn from one's mistakes. In fact, what separates the winner from the also-ran is the achiever's ability to get up again and keep heading for that goal – despite failures and setbacks along the way.

We can all take heart, in these pages, from the reflections of such great men and women as Henry Ford, Eleanor Roosevelt, George Bernard Shaw and Helen Keller, who are among the many famous people quoted here. All of them have broken through the pain barrier – and succeeded. And never forget: every one of these people started out as an unknown – with a dream.

Maggie Pinkney, 2006

BEGIN BY BELIEVING

They are able

who think

they are able.

———————————

VIRGIL, 70–19 BC
Roman poet

The thing always happens

that you really believe in;

and the belief in a thing

makes it happen.

———————

FRANK LLOYD WRIGHT, 1869–1959
American architect

The secret of making something

work in your lives is first of all,

the deep desire to make it work;

then the faith and belief that it can work;

then to hold that clear definite vision in your

consciousness and see it working out step by step,

without one thought of doubt or disbelief.

EILEEN CADDY
Co-founder of the Findhorn Foundation, Scotland

One of the greatest

of all principles is that

men can do what they

think they can do.

———————

NORMAN VINCENT PEALE, 1898–1993
American writer and minister

I knew I was going to be a comedian

when I was about six.

You get what you believe you'll get.

You have to really want it

and you'll get it.

BILLY CONNELLY, b 1942
Scottish comedian

Believe that life is worth living,

and your belief

will help create the fact.

———————

WILLIAM JAMES, 1842–1910
American psychologist and philosopher

To accomplish great things

we must not only act,

but also dream;

not only plan,

but also believe.

ANATOLE FRANCE, 1844–1924
French writer

Whether you believe

you can do a thing

or believe you can't,

you are right.

———————

HENRY FORD, 1863–1947
American car manufacturer

Believe you can, and you can.

Belief is one of the most powerful of all problem dissolvers. When you believe that a difficulty can be overcome, you are more than halfway to victory over it already.

NORMAN VINCENT PEALE, 1898–1993
American writer and minister

ALWAYS BE YOURSELF

Always be

a first-rate version of yourself,

instead of a second-rate version

of somebody else.

———————

JUDY GARLAND, 1922–1969
American singer

I was born
a jackdaw;
why should I be
an owl?

OGDEN NASH, 1902–1971
American humorous poet

What is right for one soul

may not be right for another.

It may mean having to stand on your own and

do something strange in the eyes of others.

But do not be daunted.

Do whatever it is because you know within

it is right for you.

———————

EILEEN CADDY
Co-founder of the Findhorn Foundation, Scotland

Every individual

has a place to fill in the world,

and is important, in some respect,

whether he chooses to be or not.

NATHANIEL HAWTHORNE, 1804–1864
American novelist

If I try to be like him,
who will be like me?

JEWISH PROVERB

To be nobody but yourself —

in a world which is doing its best,

night and day,

to make you like everybody else —

means to fight the hardest battle

which any human being can fight,

and never stop fighting.

E.E. CUMMINGS, 1894–1962
American poet

This above all — to thine own self be true,

And it must follow, as night follows day,

Thou canst not then be false to any man.

———————

WILLIAM SHAKESPEARE, 1564–1616
English playwright and poet

Don't surrender your individuality,

which is your greatest agent of power,

to the customs and conventionalities that

have got their life from the great mass.

Do you want to be a power in the world?

Then be yourself.

RALPH WALDO TRINE, 1866–1958
American poet and writer

What's man's first duty?

The answer's brief:

to be himself.

HENRIK IBSEN, 1828–1906
Norwegian writer, dramatist and poet

It isn't until you come to a
spiritual understanding of who you are —
not necessarily a religious feeling,
but deep down, the spirit within —
that you can begin to take control.

———————

OPRAH WINFREY, b.1954
American television personality

Resolve to be thyself;

and know that he

Who finds himself,

loses his misery.

MATTHEW ARNOLD, 1822–1888
English poet, essayist and educationalist

Being myself

includes taking risks with myself,

taking risks on new behavior,

trying new ways of 'being myself',

so that I can see who it is

I want to be.

———————————

HUGH PRATHER, b. 1938
American writer

One has just to be oneself.

That's my basic message.

The moment you accept yourself as you are,

all burdens, all mountainous burdens,

simply disappear.

Then life is a sheer joy,

a festival of lights.

BHAGWAN SHREE RAJNEESH, 1931–1990
Indian spiritual master

HOLD ON TO YOUR DREAMS

Go confidently

in the direction of your dreams!

Live the life you've imagined.

HENRY DAVID THOREAU, 1817–1862
American writer

It seems to me we can never

give up longing and wishing for things

while we are thoroughly alive.

There are certain things we feel

to be beautiful and good,

and we must hunger after them.

———————

GEORGE ELIOT (MARY ANN EVANS), 1819–1880
English novelist

All big men are dreamers. They see things in the soft haze of a spring day or in the red fire of a long winter's evening. Some of us let great dreams die, but others nourish and protect them, nurse them through bad days till they bring them to the sunshine and light which comes always to those who sincerely hope that their dreams will come true.

———————

WOODROW WILSON, 1856–1924
President of the United States of America

The future belongs to
those who believe in the
beauty of their dreams.

ELEANOR ROOSEVELT, 1884–1962
First Lady of the United States of America, writer and diplomat

Those who dream by day

are cognizant of many things

which escape those

who dream only by night.

EDGAR ALLAN POE, 1809–1849
American poet and writer

Always live your life

with one dream to fulfill.

No matter how many of your dreams

you have realized in the past,

always have a dream to go.

Because when you stop dreaming,

life becomes a mundane existence.

———————

SARA HENDERSON, 1936–2005
Australian outback station manager and writer

Some men see things as they are

and say 'Why?'

I dream things that never were

and say 'Why not?'

———————

GEORGE BERNARD SHAW, 1856–1950
Irish dramatist, essayist and critic

ATTITUDE CAN
SHAPE YOUR LIFE

It is worth

a thousand pounds a year

to have the habit of looking

on the bright side of things.

───────

SAMUEL JOHNSON, 1709–1784
English Lexicographer, critic and essayist

No pessimist ever

discovered the secrets of the stars,

or sailed to an uncharted land,

or opened a new heaven

to the horizon of the spirit.

HELEN KELLER, 1880–1968
American writer and scholar

The mind is its own place,

and in itself

can make a heaven of hell,

a hell of heaven.

———————

JOHN MILTON, 1606–1674
English poet

The greater part

of our happiness or misery

depends on our dispositions

and not on our circumstances.

We carry the seeds of the one or the other

about with us in our minds wherever we go.

MARTHA WASHINGTON, 1731–1802
First Lady of the United States of America

Make the most

of the best

and the least

of the worst.

ROBERT LOUIS STEVENSON, 1850–1894
Scottish writer and poet

A positive thinker does not

refuse to recognize the negative,

he refuses to dwell on it.

Positive thinking

is a form of thought which habitually

looks for the best results

from the worst conditions.

———————

NORMAN VINCENT PEALE, 1898–1993
American writer and minister

Over the winter glaciers

I see the summer glow;

And through the wild-piled snowdrift

The warm rosebuds below.

———————————

RALPH WALDO EMERSON, 1803–1882
American essayist and poet

In the midst of winter,

I finally learned there was in me

an invincible summer.

—————————————

ALBERT CAMUS, 1913–1960
French writer

The greatest revolution of our generation

is the discovery that human beings,

by changing the inner attitudes of their minds,

can change the outer aspects of their lives.

WILLIAM JAMES, 1842–1910
American psychologist and philosopher

THE POWER OF
ENTHUSIASM

You can do anything if you have enthusiasm. Enthusiasm is the yeast that makes your hopes rise to the stars. Enthusiasm is the spark in your eye, the swing in your gait, the grip of your hand, the irresistible surge of your will, and energy to execute your ideas …

Enthusiasm is at the bottom of all progress!

HENRY FORD, 1863–1947
American car manufacturer

If you are not getting

as much from life as you want to

then examine the state of

your enthusiasm.

NORMAN VINCENT PEALE, 1898–1993
American writer and minister

I prefer the folly of

enthusiasm to the

indifference of wisdom.

———————

ANATOLE FRANCE, 1844–1924
French writer and critic

As life is action and passion,

it is required of man

that he should share the action

and passion of his time,

at peril of being judged

not to have lived.

OLIVER WENDELL HOLMES, 1809–1894
American writer and physician

The love of life is necessary

to the vigorous prosecution

of any undertaking.

SAMUEL JOHNSON, 1709–1784
English lexicographer, critic and essayist

Live all you can:

it's a mistake not to.

It doesn't matter

what you do in particular,

so long as you have had your life.

If you haven't had that,

what have you had?

———————

HENRY JAMES, 1843–1916
American novelist

Develop interest in life as you see it;

in people, things, literature, music —

the world is so rich,

simply throbbing with rich treasures,

beautiful souls and interesting people.

Forget yourself.

———————

HENRY MILLER, 1891–1980
American author

We act as though comfort and luxury

were the chief requirements of life,

when all we need to make us really happy

is something to be enthusiastic about.

———————

CHARLES KINGSLEY, 1819–1875
English writer and clergyman

You must learn day by day,

year by year,

to broaden your horizons.

The more things you love,

the more you are interested in,

the more you enjoy,

the more you are indignant about,

the more you have left

if anything happens.

ETHEL BARRYMORE, 1879–1959
American actress

SHOOT FOR THE MOON

Far away there in the sunshine

are my highest aspirations.

I may not reach them

but I can look up and see their beauty,

believe in them and try

to follow them.

LOUISA MAY ALCOTT, 1832–1888
American novelist

Shoot for the moon.
Even if you miss it
you will land among
the stars.

LESTER LOUIS BROWN, b. 1928
American journalist

If you aspire to the highest place,

it is no disgrace to stop

at the second or even

the third place.

CICERO, 106–43 BC
Roman orator, statesman and essayist

Set your sights high,

the higher the better.

Expect the most wonderful things to happen,

not in the future but right now.

Realize that nothing is too good.

Allow absolutely nothing to hamper you

or hold you up in any way.

EILEEN CADDY
Co-founder of the Findhorn Foundation, Scotland

Our aspirations
are our
possibilities.

SAMUEL JOHNSON, 1709–1784
English lexicographer, critic and essayist

Never look down

to test the ground

before taking your next step;

only he who keeps his eye

fixed on the far horizon

will find his right road.

———————

DAG HAMMARSKJÖLD, 1905–1961
Swedish statesman and Secretary-General of the United States of America

When goals go,

meaning goes.

When meaning goes,

purpose goes.

When purpose goes,

life goes dead on our hands.

―――――――――

CARL JUNG, 1875–1961
Swiss psychiatrist

PROBLEMS ARE FOR SOLVING

If there were nothing

wrong in the world,

there wouldn't be

anything for us to do.

———————

GEORGE BERNARD SHAW, 1856–1950
Irish dramatist, essayist and critic

I'm grateful for all my problems.

As each of them was overcome

I became stronger and more able

to meet those yet to come.

I grew on my difficulties.

J.C. PENNY, 1875–1971
American retailing magnate

A problem
well stated is
a problem
half solved.

CHARLES FRANKLIN KETTERING, 1876–1958
American engineer and inventor

Problems are a major part of life.

Don't whinge about why

you always have problems …

Get on with the solving.

Take it from someone who has been there –

the solving gets easier

as you go along.

SARA HENDERSON, 1936–2005
Australian outback station manager and writer

I think these difficult time have helped me

to understand better than before

how infinitely rich and beautiful life is

in every way, and that so many things

one goes around worrying about

are of no importance whatsoever.

ISAK DINESEN (KAREN BLIXEN), 1885–1962
Danish writer

Those things that hurt, instruct.

BENJAMIN FRANKLIN, 1706–1790
American statesman and scientist

Life affords no higher pleasure

than that of surmounting difficulties,

passing from one step of success to another,

forming new wishes

and seeing them gratified.

SAMUEL JOHNSON, 1709–1784
English lexicographer, critic and essayist

Problems call forth

our courage and our wisdom; indeed,

they create our courage and our wisdom.

It is only because of problems

that we grow mentally and spiritually.

It is through the pain of

confronting and resolving problems

that we learn.

M. SCOTT PECK, b. 1936
American psychiatrist and writer

I could do nothing without my problems;

they toughen my mind.

In fact I tell my assistants not to bring me

their successes for they weaken me;

but rather to bring me their problems,

for they strengthen me.

CHARLES FRANKLIN KETTERING, 1876–1958
American engineer and inventor

RISK NOTHING –
RISK EVERYTHING!

Risk! Risk anything!

Care no more for the opinions of others,

for those voices.

Do the hardest thing on earth for you.

Act for yourself.

Face the truth.

KATHERINE MANSFIELD, 1888–1923
New Zealand writer

And the trouble is,

if you don't risk anything,

you risk even more.

ERICA JONG, b. 1942
American novelist and poet

And the day came

when the risk

to remain in a tight bud

was more painful

than the risk it took

to bloom.

———————————

ANAÏS NIN, 1903–1977
French novelist

He that is over-cautious
will accomplish little.

FRIEDRICH VON SCHILLER, 1759–1805
German historian and poet

Take calculated risks.

This is quite different

from being rash.

GEORGE S. PATTON, 1885–1945
Amrican military leader

I would not creep along the coast

but steer out in mid-sea,

by guidance of the stars.

GEORGE ELIOT (MARY ANN EVANS), 1819–1880
English novelist

There are risks and costs
to a program of action,
but they are far less than
the long-range risks and costs
of comfortable inaction.

JOHN F. KENNEDY, 1917–1963
President of the United States of America

A lot of successful people are risk-takers.

Unless you're willing to do that –

to have a go, fail miserably,

and have another go,

success won't happen.

PHILLIP ADAMS, b. 1939
Australian writer and radio broadcaster

Take chances, make mistakes.

That's how you grow.

Pain nourishes your courage.

You have to fail in order

to practice being brave.

———————

MARY TYLER MOORE, b. 1937
American actress

Risk is what separates
the good part of life
from the tedium.

JIMMY ZERO
American comedian

During the first period

of a man's life,

the danger is

not to take the risk.

SOREN KIERKGAARD, 1813–1855
Danish philosopher

Much of the satisfying work of life

begins as an experiment;

no experiment is ever

quite a failure.

_____

ALICE WALKER, b. 1944
American author

No man is worth his salt

who is not ready at all times

to risk his body,

to risk his well-being,

to risk his life

to a great cause.

MAKE THE MOST
OF YOUR MISTAKES

Some of the best lessons we ever learn,

we learn from our mistakes and failures.

The error of the past is the success

and wisdom of the future.

TYRON EDWARDS, 1861–1941
American theologian

I have learned more

from my mistakes

than from

my successes.

SIR HUMPHRY DAVY, 1778–1892
English chemist and inventor

When we begin

to take our failures non-seriously,

it means we are ceasing to be afraid of them.

It is of immense importance to learn

to laugh at ourselves.

KATHERINE MANSFIELD, 1888–1923
New Zealand short story writer

If you have made mistakes …

there is always another chance for you.

You may have a fresh start

at any moment you choose,

for this thing we call 'failure'

is not the falling down,

but the staying down.

———————

MARY PICKFORD, 1893–1979
American actress

Anyone

who has never made a mistake

has never tried anything new.

ALBERT EINSTEIN, 1879–1955
German-born American physicist

Even a mistake may turn out to be

the one thing necessary to a

worthwhile achievement.

HENRY FORD, 1863–1947
American car manufacturer

We learn wisdom from failure
much more than success.
We often discover what we WILL do,
by finding out what we will NOT do.

———————

SAMUEL SMILES, 1812–1904
Scottish author and social reformer

You know,

by the time you've reached my age,

you've made plenty of mistakes

if you've lived your life properly.

RONALD REAGAN, 1911–2004
President of the Untied States of America

Nobody makes

a greater mistake

than he who does nothing

because he could do so little.

EDMUND BURKE, 1729–1797
British politician

JUST DO IT!

I have spent my days

stringing and unstringing my instrument,

while the song I came to sing

remains unsung.

RABINDRANATH TAGORE, 1861–1941
Indian poet and philosopher

Do the thing
and you will have
the power.

RALPH WALDO EMERSON, 1803–1882
American essayist and poet

Our great business in life

is not to see what lies

dimly at a distance,

but to do what lies

clearly at hand.

———————

THOMAS CARLYLE, 1795–1881
Scottish essayist, historian and philosopher

You can't build a reputation

on what you're going to do.

HENRY FORD, 1863–1947
American car manufacturer

Don't be afraid

to take a big step

if one is indicated.

You can't cross a chasm

in two small jumps.

———————

DAVID LLOYD GEORGE, 1863–1945
British Prime Minister and statesman

Action
is the antidote
to despair.

JOAN BAEZ, b. 1941
American folk singer

Action may not always

bring happiness,

but there is no happiness

without action.

BENJAMIN DISRAELI, 1804–1881
British Prime Minister and writer

The great end of life is not knowledge, but action.

THOMAS FULLER, 1608–1661
English clergyman and writer

Sometimes

the only way for me to find out

what it is I want to do

is go ahead and do something.

Then the moment I start to act,

my feelings become clear.

HUGH PRATHER, b. 1938
American writer

Don't wait for a light to appear

at the end of the tunnel,

stride down there ... and

light the bloody thing yourself.

SARA HENDERSON, 1936–2005
Australian outback station manager and writer

A little knowledge that acts

is worth infinitely more

than knowledge that is idle.

KAHLIL GIBRAN, 1883–1931
Lebanese Poet, artist and mystic

NEVER GIVE UP

When I was a young man,

I observed that nine

out of ten things I did were failures.

I didn't want to be a failure,

so I did ten times more work.

———————

GEORGE BERNARD SHAW, 1856–1950
Irish dramatist, writer and critic

Character consists

of what you do on the

third and fourth tries.

JAMES A. MICHENER, 1907–1997
American writer

We haven't failed.

We now know a thousand things

that won't work,

so we're that much closer

to finding what will.

———————

THOMAS EDISON, 1847–1931
American inventor

Nothing in this world

can take the place of persistence.

Talent will not; nothing is more common

than unsuccessful men with talent.

Genius will not; unrewarded genius

is almost a proverb.

Education will not;

the world is full of educated failures.

Persistence and determination alone

are omnipotent.

CALVIN COOLIDGE, 1872–1933
President of the United States of America

To keep a lamp burning
we have to
keep putting oil in it.

MOTHER TERESA OF CALCUTTA, 1910–1997
Yugoslav-born missionary

When you get into a tight place

and everything goes against you,

till it seems as though you

could not hang on a minute longer,

never give up then, for that is just the

place and time that the tide will turn.

———————

HARRIET BEECHER STOWE, 1811–1896
American author and social reformer

Consider the postage stamp;

its usefulness consists

in the ability to stick to

one thing till it gets there.

———————

JOSH BILLINGS, 1818–1885
American writer

FACE UP TO FEAR

Fear is a question.

What are you afraid of and why?

Our fears are a treasure house of

self-knowledge if we explore them.

MARILYN FRENCH, b. 1929
American novelist

I have a lot of things

to prove to myself.

One is that I can live

my life fearlessly.

OPRAH WINFREY, b. 1954
American television personality

Courage faces fear

and thereby masters it.

Cowardice represses fear and

is thereby mastered by it.

———————

MARTIN LUTHER KING, JR., 1929–1968
American civil rights leader and minister

Life shrinks or expands
in proportion
to one's courage.

ANAÏS NIN, 1903–1977
French novelist

Do the thing you fear

and the death of fear

is certain.

RALPH WALDO EMERSON, 1803–1882
American essayist and poet

Life is either a daring adventure

or nothing.

To keep our faces toward change,

and behave like free spirits

in the presence of fate,

is strength undefeatable.

HELEN KELLER, 1880–1968
American writer and scholar

Facing it,
always facing it.
That's the way to get through.
Face it.

———————

JOSEPH CONRAD, 1856–1924
Polish-born British writer

Of all the liars in the world,

sometimes the worst are

your own fears.

RUDYARD KIPLING, 1865–1936
English poet and author

Within a system

which denies the existence of basic human rights,

fear tends to be the order of the day.

Yet even under the most crushing state machinery,

courage rises up again and again,

for fear is not the natural state of civilised man.

———————

AUNG SAN SUU KYI, b. 1945
Burma's democratically elected leader

I believe anyone can conquer fear

by doing the things he fears to do,

provided he keeps on doing them

until he gets a record of

successful experiences behind him.

ELEANOR ROOSEVELT, 1884–1962
First Lady of the United States of America, writer and diplomat

Courage
is resistance to fear,
mastery of fear,
not absence of fear.

MARK TWAIN, 1835–1910
American writer and humorist

When I became ill,

the years of pain and confusion loomed up like some

primitive monster of the deep…I lived in fear of dying.

The strange paradox is that by confronting my fear of

death, I found myself and created a new life.

LUCIA CAPACCHIONE
American art therapist

The bravest thing you can do

when you are not brave

is to profess courage

and act accordingly.

———————

CORRA MAY WHITE HARRIS, 1869–1935
American writer

OPPORTUNITIES ARE FOR TAKING

Grab a chance

and you won't be sorry

for a might-have-been.

———————

ARTHUR RANSOME, 1884–1967
British novelist

God helps those that help themselves.

BENJAMIN FRANKLIN, 1706–1790
American statesman and scientist

There is no security

on this earth;

there is only opportunity.

DOUGLAS MACARTHUR, 1880–1964
American military leader

There is a tide in the affairs of men

Which, taken at the flood, leads on to fortune;

Omitted, all the voyage of their life

Is bound in shallows and miseries.

On such a full sea we are now afloat,

And we must take the current when it serves,

Or lose our ventures.

WILLIAM SHAKESPEARE, 1564–1616
English poet and playwright

Do not wait for

extraordinary circumstances

to do good;

try to use

ordinary situations.

———————

JEAN PAUL RICHTER, 1763–1825
German novelist

If your ship

doesn't come in,

swim out to it.

ANONYMOUS

A wise man
makes more opportunities
than he finds.

FRANCIS BACON, 1561–1626
English philosopher

If you wait for

opportunities to

occur you will be

one of the crowd

———————

EDWARD DE BONO
American writer and exponent of creative thinking

To improve

the golden moment of opportunity,

and catch the good

that is within our reach,

is the great art of life.

WILLIAM JAMES, 1842–1910
American psychologist and philosopher

GENIUS OR
HARD WORK?

A genius!

For thirty-seven years

I've practiced fourteen hours a day,

and now they call me a genius!

———————

PABLO SARASATE, 1844–1908
Spanish violinist and composer

The secret of genius

is to carry the spirit of the child

into old age,

which means never losing

your enthusiasm.

———————————————

ALDOUS HUXLEY, 1894–1963
English writer

Genius
is nothing but labor
and diligence.

WILLIAM HOGARTH, 1697–1764
English painter and political caricaturist

Every production

of genius

must be the production

of enthusiasm.

———————

BENJAMIN DISRAELI, 1804–1881
English Prime Minister and writer

To believe your own thought,

to believe that what is

true for you in your private heart

is true for all men – that is genius.

RALPH WALDO EMERSON, 1803–1882
American essayist and poet

Genius is one percent

inspiration

and ninety-nine percent

perspiration.

THOMAS A. EDISON, 1847–1931
American inventor

Men give me credit for some genius.

All the genius I have is this:

when I have a subject in mind,

I study it profoundly.

Day and night it is before me.

My mind becomes pervaded with it …

the effort which I have made

is what people are pleased to call genius.

It is the fruit of labor and thought.

ALEXANDER HAMILTON, 1755–1804
American statesman

One is not born a genius, one becomes a genius.

SIMONE DE BEAUVOIR, 1908–1986
French writer

If people knew

how hard I work

to gain my mastery,

it would not seem

so wonderful at all.

MICHELANGELO, 1475–1564
Italian painter and sculptor

YOU CAN DO MORE THAN
YOU THINK YOU CAN

Love not
what you are
but what
you may become.

MIGUEL DE CERVANTES, 1547–1616
Spanish writer

If we did all the things

we are capable of doing

we would truly

astound ourselves.

———

THOMAS EDISON, 1847–1931
American inventor

We should say to each [child]:

Do you know what you are?

You are a marvel. You are unique…

You may become a Shakespeare,

a Michelangelo, a Beethoven.

You have the capacity

for anything.

PABLO CASALS, 1876–1973
Spanish cellist, conductor and composer

I have tried to write the best I can;

sometimes I have good luck

and write better than I can.

ERNEST HEMINGWAY, 1898–1961
American writer

No matter what

your level of ability,

you have more potential

than you can ever develop

in a lifetime.

ANONYMOUS

Compared to what we ought to be

we are only half awake.

We are making use of only a small part

of our physical and mental resources.

Stating the thing broadly,

the human individual thus lives

far within his limits.

He possesses power of various sorts

which he habitually fails to use.

WILLIAM JAMES, 1842–1910
American psychologist and philosopher

I tell you that as long

as I can conceive

something better than myself

I cannot be easy

unless I am striving to

bring it into existence

or clearing the way for it.

GEORGE BERNARD SHAW, 1856–1950
Irish dramatist, writer and critic

To be what we are,

and to become what we

are capable of becoming

is the only end in life.

ROBERT LOUIS STEVENSON, 1850–1894
Scottish author and poet

There's only one corner of the universe

you can be certain of improving,

and that's your own self.

——————

ALDOUS HUXLEY, 1894–1963
English writer

CHERISH YOUR
FRIENDS

We are all travelers

in the wilderness of this world,

and the best we can find in our travels

is an honest friend.

———————————

ROBERT LOUIS STEVENSON, 1850–1894
Scottish writer and poet

I have learned that a good friend

is the purest of all God's gifts,

for it is a love that has

no exchange or payment.

FRANCES FARMER, 1910–1970
American actress and singer

I want someone to laugh with me,

someone to be grave with me,

someone to please me and help my

discrimination with his or her remark,

and at times, no doubt, to admire

my acuteness and penetration.

ROBERT BURNS, 1759–1796
Scottish poet

Under the magnetism of friendship

the modest man becomes bold;

the shy, confident; the lazy, active;

or the impetuous,

prudent and peaceful.

WILLIAM MAKEPEACE THACKERAY, 1811–1863
English writer

Each new friend

represents a world in us,

a world possibly not born

until they arrive, and it is

only by this meeting

that a new world is born.

ANAÏS NIN, 1903–1977
French novelist

A real friend

is one who walks in

when the rest of the world

walks out.

───────────

WALTER WINCHELL, 1879–1972
American journalist

We take care of our health,

we lay up money,

we make our room tight,

and out clothing sufficient;

but who provides wisely

that he shall not be wanting in

the best property of all – friends?

RALPH WALDO EMERSON, 1803–1882
American essayist and poet

And in the sweetness of friendship

let there by laughter,

and sharing of pleasures.

For in the dew of little things

the heart finds its morning

and is refreshed.

———————————

KAHIL GIBRAN, 1883–1931
Lebanese poet, artist and mystic

Friendship

improves happiness

and abates misery

by doubling our joy

and dividing our grief.

JOSEPH ADDISON, 1672–1719
English essayist

SECRETS OF SUCCESS

Singleness of purpose

is one of the chief essentials

for success in life,

no matter what may be

one's aims.

———————

JOHN D. ROCKEFELLER, JR., 1874–1960
American oil millionaire and philanthropist

The men I have seen succeed

have always been cheerful and hopeful,

who went about their business

with a smile of their faces,

and took all the changes and chances

to this mortal life like a man.

CHARLES KINGSLEY, 1819–1875
English writer, poet and clergyman

I cannot give you

the formula for success,

but I can give you the formula

for failure — which is:

try to please everybody.

HERBERT BAYARD SWOPE, 1882–1958
American newspaper editor

Success is to be measured

not so much by the position

one has reached in life,

as by the obstacles which

one has overcome

while trying to succeed.

———————————

BOOKER T. WASHINGTON, 1856–1915
American teacher and writer

There is only one success –
to be able to spend your life
in your own way.

CHRISTOPHER DARLINGTON MORLEY, 1890–1957
American novelist and essayist

Our problem is that we make the mistake of comparing ourselves with other people. You are not inferior or superior to any human being… You do not determine your success by comparing yourself to others, rather you determine your success by comparing your accomplishments to your capabilities. You are 'number one' when you do the best you can with what you have.

ZIG SIGLAR
American motivational writer

What's money?

A man is a success

if he gets up in the morning

and goes to bed at night

and in between

does when he wants to do.

BOB DYLAN, b.1941
American singer and songwriter

Do your work
with your whole heart
and you will succeed –
there is so little competition.

ELBERT HUBBARD, 1865–1915
American writer

There are two kinds of success.

One is the very rare kind that comes to the man who has the power to do what no one else has the power to do. That is genius. But the average man who wins what we call success is not a genius. He is a man who has merely the ordinary qualities that he shares with his fellows, but who has developed those ordinary qualities to a more than ordinary degree.

———

THEODORE ROOSEVELT, 1858–1919
President of the United States of America

One only gets to the top rung of the ladder

by steadily climbing up, one at a time,

and suddenly all sorts of powers,

all sorts of abilities which you thought

never belonged to you –

suddenly become within

your own possibility and you think,

'Well, I'll have a go, too.'

———————

MARGARET THATCHER, b. 1925
British Prime Minister

Success is not about money and power.

Real success is about relationships.

There's no point in making $50 million a year

if your teenager thinks you're a jerk

and you spend no time with your wife.

CHRISTOPHER REEVE, 1952–2005
American screen actor

Self-trust
is the first secret
of success.

RALPH WALDO EMERSON, 1803–1882
American essayist and poet

My mother drew a distinction
between achievement and success.
She said that achievement is the knowledge
that you have studied and worked hard
and done the best that is in you.
Success is being praised by others.
That is nice but not as important or satisfying.
Always aim for achievement
and forget about success.

HELEN HAYES, 1900–1993
American actress

What is success?

To laugh often and much. To win the respect of
intelligent people and the affection of children.
To earn the appreciation of honest critics and endure
the betrayal of false friends. To appreciate beauty.
To find the best in others. To leave the world
a bit better, whether by a healthy child, a garden
patch or a redeemed social condition.
To know even one life breathed easier because
you have lived; this is to have succeeded.

RALPH WALDO EMERSON, 1803–1882
American essayist and poet